REDEEMED

From Poverty, Sickness,
And Spiritual Death

REDEEMED
From Poverty, Sickness, and Spiritual Death

Kenneth E. Hagin

Second Edition
Twenty-Seventh Printing 2002

ISBN 0-89276-001-X

In the U.S. write:
Kenneth Hagin Ministries
P.O. Box 50126
Tulsa, OK 74150-0126

In Canada write:
Kenneth Hagin Ministries
P.O. Box 335, Station D
Etobicoke (Toronto), Ontario
Canada, M9A 4X3

Contents

Chapter 1
Redemption From the Curse of Poverty

Christ hath redeemed us from the curse of the law, being made a curse for us: for it is written, Cursed is every one that hangeth on a tree: That the blessing of Abraham might come on the Gentiles through Jesus Christ; that we might receive the promise of the Spirit through faith. . . . And if ye be Christ's, then are ye Abraham's seed, and heirs according to the promise.

— Galatians 3:13,14,29

Christ has redeemed us from the curse of the Law!

What is the curse of the Law? The only way to find out is to go back to the Law. The expression "the Law" as found in the New Testament usually refers to the Pentateuch, the first five Books of the Bible. As we go back to these books — or the Law — we find that the curse, or punishment, for breaking God's law is threefold: poverty, sickness, and spiritual death.

1 TIMOTHY 4:8
8 For bodily exercise prof-iteth little: but godliness is profitable unto all things, having promise of the life that now is, and of that which is to come.

Some people would have us believe that we don't have any promise in this life of any blessing, material or otherwise, but this scripture emphatically declares that we do.

According to Deuteronomy 28:15-17,38-40, the curse of poverty was to come upon God's children if they disobeyed Him. It was a curse that would come upon them because they failed to observe to do all His commandments and His statutes.

Paul said, writing to the Church at Philippi, *"But my God shall supply all your need according to his riches in glory by Christ Jesus"* (Phil. 4:19). All your needs would include your financial, material, and other needs. In fact, in this chapter, Paul is talking about financial and material things.

Jesus Himself said, *"But seek ye first the kingdom of God, and his righteousness; and all these things shall be added unto you"* (Matt. 6:33). These things that shall be added unto you are material things in life — something to eat, something to wear, and so on.

Some people seem to have the idea that if a person is a Christian, a believer in God, it is a mark of humility — a mark of godliness — for him to live in poverty and not have anything. They think you ought to go through life with the top of your hat out, the soles of your shoes out, and the seat of your pants worn out — just barely able to get along.

But that isn't what Jesus said, He said, *"Seek ye first the kingdom of God, and his righteousness; and all these things shall be added unto you."* Not *taken from* you; He said they shall be *added unto* you! Praise God.

LUKE 6:38
38 Give, and it shall be given unto you; good measure, pressed down, and shaken together, and running over, shall men give into your bosom. For with the same measure that ye mete withal

it shall be measured to you again.

First, let's ask this question: Is that the truth? Did Christ speak the truth, or was He lying? I believe it is the truth, don't you? Now notice that He said, "shall men."

Of course God is behind it, but He said, "shall men give into your bosom."

I remember a friend asked me some time ago, "Brother Hagin, do you ever preach from Luke 6:38?"

"Well," I answered, "I have used the scripture. I don't know if I ever used it for a text, but I have quoted it in my preaching at various times."

This man replied, "Well, recently we had a minister in our church who preached a two-week meeting, and he referred to that scripture every night. One night he preached a sermon on it. You know, I'd never thought much about that verse until he emphasized it so much. Then, in the last service of the meeting, after our pastor had received the love offering for him, the evangelist said, 'Folks, I am impressed by the Spirit of God to receive an offering for the church here to put in an air-conditioning system.'"

My friend, who taught the men's Bible class, a large class of about 100, continued telling me about the last night's service.

"The evangelist said to the congregation of about 1,800, 'I want to get that $10,000 tonight! It sounds big, I know, and you've given during this meeting, but I want to challenge you.' He read us this text again which he'd mentioned every night, '*Give, and it shall be given unto you.*'

"Then he said, 'I don't want anybody to give anything they can afford to give. Give what you *can't* afford. If you feel you can afford to give $50 but not $100, give the $100. If you think you can afford to give $500 but not $1,000, give the $1,000. There's where the blessing is — and that's the truth.'

"Then he added, 'I'm going to lay my Bible here on the altar, and I want you to come and lay your money on this verse of Scripture and say, "Dear Lord, I'm acting on Your Word." I'll pray especially for you, but I know God is going to repay you. It will work for you. And if it doesn't, I'll see that you get your money back, and nothing will ever be said about it.'"

The Sunday school teacher said, "Brother Hagin, I had a number of businessmen in my class. Two of them had come to me before this asking me to pray because their businesses were going bankrupt. Unless God did something within 30 days, they said they'd have to close their doors."

He went on, "Brother Hagin, I'm a witness to the fact that one of these men gave $500 in that offering and the other gave $250. It was really borrowed money, but in 30 days both businesses were out of the red! God blessed them immeasurably."

In Malachi 3:10, the Lord spoke these words, *"Bring ye all the tithes into the storehouse, that there may be meat in mine house, and prove me now herewith, saith the Lord of hosts, if I will not open you the windows of heaven, and pour you out a blessing, that there shall not be room enough to receive it."*

Actually, we haven't really given until we've paid our tithes.

One fellow said to me, "Brother Hagin, paying tithes — that's just under the Old Testament. That's

just under the Mosaic Law. Didn't
you know that?"

I would hate to exhibit my
ignorance of the Bible by making
such a statement. Abraham paid
tithes 500 years before the Law
was given by Moses. Jacob paid
tithes 250 years before then.

"Yes," someone said, "but there
isn't any scripture in the New Testament about paying tithes."

Those folks ought to read.
Look at Hebrews 7:8. What about
that? That's New Testament, isn't
it? "*And here men that die receive
tithes; but there he receiveth them,
of whom it is witnessed that he
liveth.*"

That's talking about Christ.

Abraham's Blessing
Is Ours

Almost every time you get
something good from the Word of
God, or the promise of something
good and a scripture to stand on,

someone pops up and says, "That's just for the Jews. That's not for us today."

I want you to know that Abraham's blessing belongs to us. It doesn't belong only to the *physical* descendants of Abraham; it belongs to us!

Remember how our chapter text said, *"That the blessing of Abraham might come on the Gentiles through Jesus Christ. . . . And if ye be Christ's, then are ye Abraham's seed, and heirs according to the promise"* (Gal. 3:14,29).

Abraham's blessing is ours! They can't take it away from us anymore. Those doubters, unbelievers, joy-killers, and doubt-peddlers will not be able to take it away from us. Abraham's blessing is mine — Abraham's blessing is yours — through Jesus Christ! Hallelujah!

Abraham's blessing was a threefold blessing. The first thing

God promised Abraham was that He was going to make him rich.

"Do you mean God is going to make us all rich?" Yes, that's what I mean.

"Do you mean He's going to make us all millionaires?" No, I didn't say that.

But He is going to make us rich. You may not understand what the word "rich" means. The dictionary says it means "a full supply," or "abundantly provided for." Praise God, there is a full supply in Christ!

I had a new car once, but it did-n't get good gas mileage — only about 13½ miles per gallon on the open road. This particular car had a reputation of getting good gas mileage, so they gave it a motor tune-up, replaced the spark plugs and the condenser, and reworked the carburetor.

As I watched, the mechanic said to me, "Preacher, here's one thing that's wrong. I don't know why they did it, but on this model they changed the carburetor. There's a setting on the inside as well as the outside. It can be set on either rich or lean. In this case it's set on rich. It's set so as to get a full supply."

God did not promise we would have a lean supply, but a *rich* supply. We're abundantly provided for! Praise God forevermore!

I preached a meeting several years ago in a small New Jersey town for Pastor A. A. Swift of the Trinity Pentecostal Church. At that time he was 70 years of age. I wasn't preaching along these lines in those days — I would preach up to it and around it. I knew it was true, but nobody else was preaching that God had redeemed us from the curse of poverty, so I didn't know whether I should come out on it or not.

Knowing Brother Swift was a man of God, an old-timer in Pentecost considered to be one of the most outstanding Full Gospel Bible teachers, I talked to him about some of these scriptures.

"Brother Hagin, you are absolutely right," he said. "You ought to preach that everywhere you go. God has promised to make every one of us rich."

Then he said, "Let me tell you how I found out. I received the Holy Spirit in 1908, and in 1911 my wife and I went to China as missionaries. (That was way back before there was a Full Gospel organization or a Pentecostal circle.)

"I was born and grew up in London, came over to Canada, and then to the United States, so I had some connections in England, and a mission there supported us. They gave us $1,236 a year. That's $103 a month support. And we spent the year 1911, or most of it, in China as missionaries.

"But every time I would go to pray — I had a place where I went for my secret prayers — the Spirit of God would deal with my heart and tell me, 'Send in your resignation. If these people knew you believed in speaking with tongues, they wouldn't support you, because they don't believe speaking with tongues is the evidence of the baptism of the Holy Spirit. You have stayed quiet, which is almost the same as receiving the money under false pretenses. You can't preach what the Bible teaches. On the sly you may get it over to a few people, but if you come right out and preach it, that will be the end. I want you to preach the full truth.'

"Lord, what am I to do?" Brother Swift finally asked the

Lord. "If I do that, my wife and I and our children will be cut off without any support here in China. It would be rough enough to be in America without support in 1912, much less in China. What am I to do?"

God answered him, "I want you to turn this mission station back to them. It wouldn't be right for you to steal it from them. [And it wouldn't.] You go over to another place and start a new work."

"Lord, start a new work in China in 1912 with no one to support it?"

"That's what I want you to do."

"Lord, we'll never make it."

"Didn't you know I promised to make you rich?"

Brother Swift replied, "If You did, I didn't know it. But I surely would be glad to know it."

Then the Spirit of the Lord asked, "Have you read Galatians

3:13,14 where it says Christ
redeemed you from the curse of
the law, being made a curse for
you, that the blessing of Abraham
might come on the Gentiles; that
is, on you? *The first thing I
promised Abraham was that I
would make him rich."*

As Brother Swift related this,
he said to me, "Then things began
to open up to me. I got my Bible
and read it — and sure enough,
there it was! I sent in my resignation and went over to another
place and began a new work. For
the first six months, it was diffi-
cult."

Don't think there won't be trials. But just because tests come,
trials mount up, and it looks like
it isn't working doesn't mean it
isn't true. You see, God doesn't
always settle up every Saturday
night. God doesn't settle up the
first of every month. But I want to
tell you — God does settle up

sooner or later. Sooner or later there comes a payday!

Many people think they have gotten away with sin because they got away with it for one week and judgment didn't fall. They got by two weeks and judgment didn't fall. They went on a month or more and judgment didn't come. They began to feel a little easier, a little better. They said, "Well, it looks as if I got by with that." But I want to tell you, sooner or later, it is coming.

"For the first six months of that year," Brother Swift told me, "it looked as if my wife and I and our two small children were going to starve to death in China, cut off from the support in England, with nobody from America to support us. What did we do?

"Well, I stayed calm, sweet, and quiet — I didn't do a lot of praying. I simply reminded God of what His Word said. I knew He was going to do something about it.

"When the year was over and I checked up, God had given me $3,750 in American dollars!"

In 1912, $3,750 was like having $15,000 or more today. He had been getting $1,236 a year. This year he got three times as much. God promised He would make him rich. Praise God forevermore!

You know, friends, most of us are not poor because we have honored God — but because we have dishonored Him. (I've given you scriptures to prove it.)

Someone said, "Oh yes, but Brother Hagin, I'm afraid of money."

"Why?" I asked.

"The Bible says money is the root of all evil. . . ."

The Bible doesn't say that at all. The Bible says, *"For the LOVE of money is the root of all evil . . ."*

(1 Tim. 6:10). You could be guilty of that sin and not have a dime. It's not wrong to *have* money; it's wrong for money to *have you*.

If money becomes a man's master, it is wrong. A man can love money so much that he'll pick it up anywhere he goes, any way he can. If you cut off his hands, he'll get it with his toes. If you cut off his toes, he'll pick it up with his teeth. If you pull his teeth, he'll gum it. If that's in him, he'll get it. It's his master.

The Bible says that the silver and the gold are God's (Hag. 2:8). The Bible says that the cattle on a thousand hills are God's (Ps. 50:10). Why did God put all these things here, anyway? He surely didn't put them here for the devil and his gang! If He did, then He loves the devil's children more then He does His own children.

That would be like some man letting his children go hungry and not paying the rent while he goes across the street and pays some other woman's rent and feeds some other woman's children. God doesn't love the devil more than He loves us. Isn't that right?

Somebody said, "Brother, I guess I'm another Job."

What do you mean you're another Job? Praise God, if you're God's Job, you'll get your healing. Job got healed.

Some people think, "Poor old Job — he went through life sick, suffering, and afflicted."

Why, the whole Book of Job happened in nine months' time. If Job was ever sick again, we don't know it. The Bible didn't say so. And if he'd ever had anything else like that, the Bible would have said so.

God healed his body! God gave him ten more children. God gave him twice as much as he had to begin with: twice as many camels, twice as many sheep, twice as many oxen, and twice as many donkeys. And Job lived 140 more years. He lived to see his children's children until the fourth generation. Glory to God! That's the way God does things. If it's wrong to be prosperous, then God did wrong by doing all that.

PROVERBS 19:17
17 He that hath pity upon the poor lendeth unto the Lord; and that which he hath given will he pay him again.

There are always those in society who are unfortunate. God has blessed and prospered us, and He doesn't want us to be miserly. He wants us to help others, so God said, *"He that hath pity upon the poor lendeth unto the Lord."* If the Lord were to come to you today and say, "I need $100," would you loan it to Him? Or if one of your brothers were to come to you to borrow $100, would you loan it to him if you could?

"Whoever has pity on the poor lendeth to the Lord" is what the Bible says. And God said, "I'll repay him." I believe He will, don't you? I don't believe He lied about it.

Just how is He going to pay it? I don't know, but I think we can have some idea of it from Luke 5:4-7, where Christ borrowed Simon Peter's boat. He repaid Peter by giving him two shiploads of fish. There's one thing about it: There is nothing stingy about the Lord!

I want people to know that I'm on God's side. I'm on the blessing side. I'm going to take advantage of what belongs to me in Christ. And I want you to take your stand. You know now what the blessing is. Hallelujah!

Chapter 2
Redemption From the Curse of Sickness

Christ hath redeemed us from the curse of the law, being made a curse for us. . . .

— Galatians 3:13

Christ has redeemed us from the curse of the Law! Before we proceed, let's look at what the curse of the Law entails.

DEUTERONOMY 28:15-22, 27-29,35,58-61
15 But it shall come to pass, if thou wilt not hearken unto the voice of the Lord thy God, to observe to do all his commandments and his statutes which I command thee this day; that all these curses shall come upon thee, and overtake thee:

16 Cursed shalt thou be in the city, and cursed shalt thou be in the field.

17 Cursed shall be thy basket and thy store.

18 Cursed shall be the fruit of thy body, and the fruit of thy land, the increase of thy kine, and the flocks of thy sheep.

19 Cursed shalt thou be when thou comest in, and cursed shalt thou be when thou goest out.

20 The Lord shall send upon thee cursing, vexation, and rebuke, in all that thou settest thine hand unto for to do, until thou be destroyed, and until thou perish quickly; because of the wickedness of thy doings, whereby thou hast forsaken me.

21 The Lord shall make the pestilence cleave unto thee, until he have consumed thee from off the land, whither thou goest to possess it.

22 The Lord shall smite thee with a consumption, and with a fever, and with an inflammation, and with an extreme burning, and with the sword, and with blasting, and with mildew; and they shall pursue thee until thou perish . . . .

27 The Lord will smite thee with the botch of Egypt, and with the emerods, and with the scab, and with the itch, whereof thou canst not be healed.

28 The Lord shall smite thee with madness, and blindness, and astonishment of heart:

29 And thou shalt grope at noonday, as the blind gropeth in darkness, and thou shalt not prosper in thy ways: and thou shalt be only oppressed and spoiled evermore, and no man shall save thee. . . .

35 The Lord shall smite thee in the knees, and in the legs, with a sore botch that cannot be healed, from the sole

of thy foot unto the top of thy head. . . .

58 If thou wilt not observe to do all the words of this law that are written in this book, that thou mayest fear this glorious and fearful name, THE LORD THY GOD;

59 Then the Lord will make thy plagues wonderful, and the plagues of thy seed, even great plagues, and of long continuance, and sore sicknesses, and of long continuance.

60 Moreover he will bring upon thee all the diseases of Egypt, which thou wast afraid of; and they shall cleave unto thee.

61 Also every sickness, and every plague, which is not written in the book of this law, them will the Lord bring upon thee, until thou be destroyed.

We can readily see from these scriptures that sickness is a curse of the Law. The dreadful diseases enumerated here — in fact, every sickness and every disease, according to the 61st verse — are part of the punishment for breaking God's law.

The *King James Version* of these scriptures would lead us to believe that God Himself puts sickness and afflictions upon His people, for it reads, *"The Lord shall smite thee. . . ."*

Dr. Robert Young, author of *Hints to Bible Interpretation,* points out that in the original Hebrew, the verb is in the permissive rather than the causative sense. Actually, it should have been translated something like this: "The Lord will *allow* you to be smitten. . . The Lord will *allow* these plagues to be brought upon you. . . ."

Many other verbs were translated in the causative sense in the *King James Version.* For example, Isaiah 45:7 reads, *"I form the light, and create darkness: I make peace,*

*and create evil: I the Lord do all
these things." Does God create evil?*
No. That would make God a devil.
God may *permit* evil, but He does
not *create* it.

Amos 3:6 in the *King James
Version* declares, *"Shall a trumpet
be blown in the city, and the people not be afraid? shall there be
evil in a city, and the Lord hath
not done it?"* If God commits evil,
then He has no right whatsoever
to judge man for sinning. But God
has not done evil; He only permits
evil. There is a vast difference
between *commission* and *permis-
sion.*

When King Saul backslid,
First Samuel 16:14 says, *". . . the
Spirit of the Lord departed from
Saul, and an evil spirit from the
Lord troubled him."*

What actually happened was
that Saul's sin broke fellowship
with God, and God permitted the

evil spirit from the devil to trouble him.

The original Hebrew of these scriptures was in the permissive tense, but because the English language has no corresponding permissive tense, the verbs were translated in the causative tense.

No, God does not send plagues and sickness upon His people as these verses seem to indicate. God's Word does not teach that these things come directly from God.

When God's people broke His commandments, they no longer were under His divine protection. All He could do was permit the devil to bring those afflictions upon them. Their sin and wrongdoing brought those dreadful plagues upon them.

Deuteronomy 28 lists several diseases in the curse of the broken law. Among them are: pestilence, consumption (tuberculosis), fever (including all types, such as typhus, scarlet, typhoid, smallpox and all other eruptive fevers), inflammation, extreme burning, the botch of Egypt, emerods, scab (all skin diseases), itch, madness, and blindness.

According to verse 60, we can add to this list ". . . *all the diseases of Egypt, which thou wast afraid of.*" And verse 61 makes it all-inclusive: "*Also every sickness, and every plague, which is not written in the book of the law.*"

We can conclude from these scriptures that sickness and disease are a part of the curse of the Law — and they should come upon us. But praise God, "*Christ hath redeemed us from the curse of the law . . .*" (Gal. 3:13).

Sickness: Blessing or Curse?

Is sickness a blessing or a curse? God's Word declares it is a curse. Some people would have you believe God "blesses" His children with sickness and disease. (If He does, I would prefer to let someone else have that "blessing.") But, *according to God's Word, sickness is a curse, and health is a blessing!*

Disease is *broken ease*. Sickness is pain and suffering. It makes slaves of family and friends who must care for sick loved ones. Disease and sickness are enemies of mankind.

Sickness is a thief and a robber. It has robbed many a young mother of her health, beauty, and joy. It has robbed her husband of his wife, and has deprived her children of their mother, for she is no longer able to fulfill the duties of a wife and mother.

Disease has robbed many young men, coming upon them in the midst of young manhood, filling them with anxiety and fear, robbing them of faith.

Sickness and disease rob people of happiness, health, and money which is needed for other things.

Sickness: Is It God's Will?

Sickness and disease are not the will of God for His people. He does not want a curse to be upon His children because of their disobedience; He wants to bless them with health.

"Oh, yes," some people have said to me, "I believe God was Israel's Healer under the Old Covenant, and He wanted the children of Israel to have health, but we're not living under that covenant."

That's true. But if the Old Covenant provided for healing and the New Covenant (or Testament) does not, I wonder if the

New Covenant is as good as the old? Thank God, the Bible says that the New Covenant is *better:*

HEBREWS 8:6
6 But now hath he obtained a more excellent ministry, by how much also he is the mediator of a BETTER covenant, which was established upon BETTER promises.

Let me remind you that our text is from the New Testament: *"Christ hath redeemed us from the curse of the law, being made a curse for us . . ."* (Gal. 3:13).

It is not the will of God that we be sick. In Bible days, it was not God's will for the children of Israel to be sick, and they were God's *servants.* Today, we are God's *children.* If it was not His will for even His servants to be sick, it could not be His will for His children to be sick! Sickness and disease are not of love. God is love.

In Luke 13, Jesus was teaching in one of the synagogues on the sabbath. A woman came in who was bent over. She could have had arthritis or something of that nature, because her body was bent in a stationary position. Jesus called her to Him and said, ". . . *Woman, thou art loosed from thine infirmity*" (v. 12).

When the ruler of the synagogue became angry because Christ healed the sick woman, Jesus said, *"Ought not this woman, being a daughter of Abraham, whom Satan hath bound, lo, these eighteen years, be loosed from this bond on the sabbath day?"* (v. 16). Jesus said it was Satan who had bound this woman.

In preaching to Cornelius' household, Peter said:

ACTS 10:38
38 How God anointed Jesus of Nazareth with the Holy Ghost and with power: who

**went about doing good, and
healing all that were
oppressed of the devil; for
God was with him.**

This scripture makes it clear
that the people Jesus healed were
oppressed of the devil.

Some people today would have
you believe that God sends sickness upon people to bless them.
They'll tell you, "Stay away from
those meetings where they pray
for the sick to be healed. That's of
the devil."

If they are right, then God and
the devil must have swapped jobs
lately! Two thousand years ago,
Satan was oppressing people and
Jesus was *healing* them.

The Bible tells us, *"Jesus
Christ the same yesterday, and to
day, and for ever"* (Heb. 13:8).
Jesus never changes! From the
beginning to the end of His public
ministry, Christ was combatting
Satan. His battle was not with

men, but with demons who indwelt men.

Don't ever tell anyone sickness is the will of God for us. It isn't! Healing and health are the will of God for mankind. If sickness were the will of God, heaven would be filled with sickness and disease.

Remember, Jesus in His earth walk was the will of God in action. He came to unveil the Father to us. He is the Word of God. He is God speaking to us. (*See* John 1:14; Heb. 1:1,2.) If you want to know what God thinks about sickness, look at Jesus! He went about healing the sick!

ISAIAH 53:4,5
4 Surely he hath borne our griefs [sicknesses]**, and carried our sorrows** [diseases]**: yet we did esteem him stricken, smitten of God, and afflicted.**
5 But he was wounded for our transgressions, he was bruised for our iniquities:

the chastisement of our peace was upon him; and with his stripes we are healed.

Matthew quotes a portion of these scriptures:

MATTHEW 8:17
17 That it might be fulfilled which was spoken by Esaias the prophet, saying, Himself took our infirmities, and bare our sicknesses.

The Holy Spirit, looking back at Calvary, wrote in the past tense through Peter:

1 PETER 2:24
24 Who his own self bare our sins in his own body on the tree, that we, being dead to sins, should live unto right-eousness: by whose stripes ye were healed.

I read from the pen of Dr. John Alexander Dowie about how he received light on the subject of healing.[1]

Dr. Dowie was pastor of a Congregational church in Newtown, a suburb of Sydney, Australia, when the bubonic plague struck there around 1875. People were dying like flies. Dr. Dowie buried forty members of his congregation in less than a month. Four more died and were yet to be buried, and many more were stricken with the plague. There was no cure.

After visiting the many sick members of his flock one day, Dr. Dowie returned home and sat in his study, his arms folded upon his desk, his head upon his arms, weeping before God.

"God, is everybody going to die?" he cried. "Are You going to take everybody? Where did this plague come from? Are You the author of this?" He was heartsick at the thought of the families that would be torn apart by the plague

— at the children who would be left orphans.

Dr. Dowie wrote many years later: "Then the words of the Holy Ghost inspired in Acts 10:38 stood before me all radiant with light, revealing Satan as the Defiler, and Christ as the Healer.

"My tears were wiped away," Dr. Dowie said. "My heart was strong. I saw the way of healing, and the door thereto was opened wide, so I said, 'God, help me now to preach the Word to all the dying around, and tell them how 'tis Satan that still defiles, and Jesus still delivers, for "He is just the same today."'"

He did not have long to wait. Within minutes, two young men burst into his study, pleading breathlessly, "Oh, come at once. Mary is dying!" Dr. Dowie ran down the street after them, not even pausing to take his hat. He was furious that Satan should have attacked this innocent young member of his flock.

Dr. Dowie entered Mary's room and found her in convulsions. Her medical doctor, having given up on her, was preparing to leave. He turned to Dr. Dowie and remarked, "Sir, are not God's ways mysterious?"

The revelation Dr. Dowie had just received from the Word of God was burning in his heart. "*God's* way!" he thundered. "How *dare* you call that God's way! No, sir, that is *the devil's* work!"

He challenged the physician, who was a member of his congregation, "Can you pray the prayer of faith that saves the sick?"

The doctor replied, "You are much too excited, sir, 'tis best to say God's will be done," and he left.

"Excited!" Dr. Dowie wrote. "The word was quite inadequate,

for I was almost frenzied with Divinely imparted anger and hatred of that foul destroyer, Disease, which was doing Satan's will.

"'It is not so,' I exclaimed. 'No will of God sends such cruelty, and I shall never say "God's will be done" to Satan's works, which God's own Son came to destroy, and this is one of them.' Oh, how the Word of God was burning in my heart. . . ."

Furious at Satan's attack, Dr. Dowie prayed the prayer of faith for Mary. Years later, he said he prayed something like this:

"Our Father, help! Holy Spirit, teach me how to pray. Plead thou for us, oh, Jesus, Saviour, Healer, Friend, our Advocate with God the Father. Hear and heal, Eternal One! From all disease and death deliver this sweet child of Thine. I rest upon the Word. We claim the promise now. The Word is true, 'I am the Lord that healeth thee.' Then heal her now. The Word is true, 'I am the Lord, I change not.' Unchanging God, then prove Thyself the Healer now. The Word is true. 'These signs shall follow them that believe. In My Name, they shall lay hands on the sick, and they shall recover.' And I believe, and I lay hands in Jesus' Name on her, and claim this promise now. Thy Word is true. 'The prayer of faith shall save the sick.' Trusting in Thee alone, I cry, oh, save her now, for Jesus' sake, Amen!"

The girl's convulsions ceased immediately, and she fell into such a deep sleep that her mother feared she had died. "She isn't dead," the triumphant Dr. Dowie assured them. "I saw that Christ had heard and that once more, as long ago in Peter's house, 'He touched her and the fever left her.'"

After several minutes, Dr. Dowie awakened Mary. She turned to her mother and exclaimed, "Mother, I feel so well!"

Remembering how Jesus had ministered to the little girl He had raised from the dead in Bible days, Dr. Dowie asked, "And you're hungry?"

"Oh yes," she agreed. "I'm so hungry."

Dr. Dowie instructed Mary's nurse to fix her a cup of cocoa and some bread and butter. Quietly thanking God, he went into the next room, where her brother and sister lay sick with the same plague. After prayer, they, too, instantly recovered.

Dr. Dowie recalled, "As I went away from the home where Christ as the Healer had been victorious, I could not but have somewhat in my heart of the triumphant song that rang through Heaven, and yet I was not a little amazed at my own strange doings, and still more at my discovery that HE IS JUST THE SAME TODAY."

From that day on, Dr. Dowie ministered to his flock on divine healing and prayed for their healing. He never lost another member to the plague.

But isn't it strange that the doctor, who was a member of Dowie's church, would treat people and give them medicine, but when they got beyond the aid of medical science, he called it the will of God?

It puzzles me that people will take medicines and do everything they can to get well, but if you suggest they have someone pray for their healing, they'll say, "It may not be God's will to heal me."

Why didn't they question the will of God in the first place? If it isn't God's will for them to be well,

they shouldn't take any medicine
or treatment. They would be out of
God's will trying to get well!

I do not mean to discredit the
medical profession. Doctors are
fighting the same devil we are. I
merely want to point out that this
is human reasoning and wrong
thinking, and it has robbed many
people of the blessings of healing
and heath.

Dr. Lilian B. Yeomans was a
doctor who practiced medicine
and surgery many years ago in
one of New York City's largest
hospitals. She began to take small
amounts of dope to steady her
nerves and help her sleep when
she felt exhausted from overwork.
Eventually she became so depen-
dent on drugs — especially morphine — that she became an
addict. She daily took fifty times
the normal dose of morphine nor-
mally prescribed for an adult
male plus other drugs.

Although Dr. Yeomans took all the celebrated cures of her day and desperately tried to stop taking drugs, she steadily grew worse. A nurse described her as "a skeleton with a devil inside." Her friends considered her case hopeless.

Dr. Yeomans had been saved as a young woman, but had backslid. When she found herself at death's door, she immersed herself in her long-neglected Bible, got back into fellowship with God, and was healed in 1898 of the terrible drug habit that had almost claimed her life.

After receiving this healing, Dr. Yeomans preached the Gospel for forty some years. When she and her sister inherited some property, they turned it into a "faith home," taking people beyond medical help who were seeking healing for their bodies.

Dr. Yeomans said they got nearly all of these people healed by working with them until they got enough faith built up in their hearts (spirits) to receive healing from God. In one of her books she gave the following example of building faith in a patient.

One day a woman in the last stages of tuberculosis was brought to the home. Doctors had given her up as beyond medical aid. When the ambulance brought the woman in, Dr. Yeomans knew she was dying. Had she still been practicing medicine, Dr. Yeomans would have begun to administer strong drugs immediately.

Instead, the woman was carried to an upstairs room, and Dr. Yeomans began reading the Bible to her. She spent about two hours reading scriptures concerning divine healing; especially from Deuteronomy 28 and Galatians 3:13.

Then she instructed the dying woman to repeat to herself every waking moment, "According to Deuteronomy 28:22, consumption (or tuberculosis) is a curse of the law. But according to Galatians 3:13, Christ has redeemed me from the curse of the law. Therefore, I no longer have tuberculosis."

The next morning, Dr. Yeomans asked the woman if she had been repeating what she'd instructed her to say. She answered that it seemed as if she'd said it 10,000 times, but she couldn't understand what it meant. Dr. Yeomans read more scriptures to her and asked her to continue repeating the same words.

The next day the story was the same. On the third morning, the woman still did not understand. Dr. Yeomans had not even prayed with her yet, even though she'd been in her "faith home" three nights. (I think sometimes we pray for people too quickly. We should instruct them more in the Word first.)

On the afternoon of the third day, Dr. Yeomans and her sister were helping prepare the evening meal when they heard a commotion upstairs. Their new patient came rushing down the stairs, shouting at the top of her voice, "Sister Yeomans, did you know? Christ has redeemed me, and I no longer have tuberculosis! It's gone now!"

You see, Dr. Yeomans realized that the way into the heart is through the mind. She knew if the woman would say to herself often enough, "According to Deuteronomy 28:22, consumption is a curse of the law. But according to Galatians 3:13, Christ hath redeemed me from the curse of the law. Therefore, I no longer have tuberculosis," the truth eventually would register on her heart.

I challenge you to take those scriptures and insert in place of consumption the name of any disease you or a loved one desire to be healed from, because Deuteronomy 28:61 says *every sickness* is a curse of the Law. It will work for you, too.

Just before her death, Dr. Yeomans published a book of psalms, hymns, and spiritual songs called *Gold of Ophir*. These were the psalms, hymns, and spiritual songs (Col. 3:16) the Spirit of God gave to her sister.

Dr. Yeomans said that when she and her sister prayed, her sister would sing songs or psalms in tongues and then sing the interpretation. Sometimes she would sing them out of prophecy. Dr. Yeomans wrote them down and collected them into this book. One of those spiritual songs given by the Spirit of God to Dr. Yeoman's sister was based on Galatians 3:13:

> *Christ redeemed me from the curse of the law,*
>
> *As He hung on that shameful tree,*
>
> *And all that is worse is contained in the curse,*
>
> *And Jesus has set me free.*
>
> *Not under the curse, not under the curse,*
>
> *Jesus has set me free;*
>
> *For sickness, I've health; for poverty, wealth,*
>
> *Since Jesus has ransomed me.*

[1] Gordon Lindsay, *John Alexander Dowie*, (Dallas, Christ for the Nations, Inc., reprinted 1980).

Chapter 3
Redemption From the Curse of Spiritual Death

Christ hath redeemed us from the curse of the law, being made a curse for us: for it is written, Cursed is every one that hangeth on a tree: That the blessing of Abraham might come on the Gentiles through Jesus Christ; that we might receive the promise of the Spirit through faith.
— Galatians 3:13,14

The first curse which God said would come upon man for breaking His law is found in Genesis 2:17, where God said to Adam, ". . . *in the day that thou eatest thereof thou shalt surely die.*"

Adam and Eve were permitted to eat fruit of all the trees in the Garden of Eden except the fruit of the tree of knowledge of good and evil. The curse of spiritual death was to come upon them if they disobeyed God. Genesis 3:22-24 tells us man disobeyed God, was driven from the Garden, and could eat no longer of the tree of life. He became the slave of sin and death.

Death has always been a mystery to man. It was not a part of the creation or part of God's original plan. The Bible tells us that physical death is an enemy of God and man. First Corinthians 15:26 tells us physical death is the last enemy that shall be put under foot.

Before we can understand death, however, we must understand that man is not a physical being. Man is a spirit who possesses a soul and lives in a body (1 Thess. 5:23).

Jesus told Nicodemus, ". . . *Ye must be born again*" (John 3:7).

Nicodemus was thinking naturally when he asked, ". . . *How can a man be born when is old? can he enter the second time into his mother's womb, and be born?*" (vs. 4).

Jesus explained, *"That which is born of the flesh is flesh; and that which is born of the Spirit is spirit"* (v. 6).

The New Birth is the rebirth of the human spirit.

The real man is the spirit. The spirit operates through the soul: the intellect, sensibilities, and will. And the soul operates through the body.

The real you (your spirit) and your soul live in a physical body. When you die physically, your spirit and soul leave the body and go to your eternal home.

In Luke 16, Christ gave us the experience of the rich man and Lazarus:

LUKE 16:19-24
19 There was a certain rich man, which was clothed in purple and fine linen, and fared sumptuously every day:
20 And there was a certain beggar named Lazarus, which was laid at his gate, full of sores.
21 And desiring to be fed with the crumbs which fell from the rich man's table: moreover the dogs came and licked his sores.
22 And it came to pass, that the beggar died, and was carried by the angels into Abraham's bosom: [Notice that the angels carried *him*, not his body, but *him* — spirit and soul — to Abraham's bosom.] **the rich man also died, and was buried;**

23 And in hell he lift up his eyes, being in torments, and seeth Abraham afar off, and Lazarus in his bosom.
24 And he cried and said, Father Abraham, have mercy on me, and send Lazarus, that he may dip the tip of his finger in water, and cool my tongue; for I am tormented in this flame.

Both Lazarus and the rich man were still conscious. Man is not dead like an animal, as some would have you believe. And there is no such thing as "soul sleep."

Several kinds of death are spoken of in the Bible, but there are three kinds we need to familiarize ourselves with: (1) spiritual death; (2) physical death; (3) eternal death, or the second death, which is being cast into the lake that burns with fire and brimstone.

Spiritual death is that which lays hold of our spirits rather than our bodies. The second death is the ultimate finality of death, or the home of the spiritually dead.

Physical death in mankind is a result of spiritual death.

In other words, spiritual death came to earth first, then manifested itself in the physical body by destroying it. Physical death is a manifestation of the law which is at work within. Paul called it *"the law of sin and death"* (Rom. 8:2).

When God said to Adam, *". . . in the day that thou eatest thereof thou shalt surely die"* (Gen. 2:7), He did not refer to physical death, but to spiritual death. If man never had died spiritually, he would not have died physically.

Spiritual death means separation from God.

The moment Adam sinned, he was separated from God. When God came down in the cool of the

day, as was His custom, to walk
and talk with Adam, He called,
". . . *Adam . . . Where art thou?*"
And Adam said, ". . . *I hid myself*"
(Gen. 3:9,10). He was separated
from God.

When Adam and Eve listened
to the devil, he became their spiritual father, and they had the
devil's nature in their spirits. This
is spiritual death. That nature
immediately began to manifest
itself in the human family. Eventually, Adam and Eve's firstborn son
murdered the second-born.

Man was now united with the
devil. He was an outcast, an out-
law, driven from the Garden with
no legal ground to approach God.

Man no longer responds to the
call of God. He responds only to
his new nature; his new master.
Man is more than a transgressor;
more than a lawbreaker and sinner. Man is spiritually a child of

the devil, and he partakes of his father's nature.

Jesus said to the Pharisees, "*Ye are of your father the devil, and the lusts of your father ye will do. He was a murderer from the beginning, and abode not in the truth, because there is no truth in him. When he speaketh a lie, he speaketh of his own: for he is liar, and the father of it*" (John 8:44).

The Pharisees were very religious. They went to the synagogue on the sabbath. They prayed. They paid their tithes. They fasted. They did a lot of other fine and good things. But they lied about Christ and murdered Him. Jesus said they were children of the devil. They had the characteristics of the devil.

This explains why man cannot be saved by his conduct or good works; he must be born again. If man were not a child of the devil, he could just act right and he'd be all right. But since he's a child of the devil, even if he tries to act right, he'd still go to hell when he dies — to the lake which burns with fire and brimstone, which is the second death.

Why? Man cannot stand in the Presence of God as he is, because he has the nature of his father, the devil, in him. Man had to be saved by someone's paying the penalty for his sins and giving him a new nature.

You might take a flop-eared old mule and try to make him into a racehorse, but it won't work. You can file his teeth, polish his hooves, feed him the finest food, run him around the track every day, and house him in the finest stable. On the day of the race, when the gun sounds, all he'll do is lope off down the track because he's a mule. It's just not in him — it's not in his nature — to be a racehorse.

Yet you can take a racehorse, and even with improper care, when the gun sounds, he's gone! It's his nature. He's born and bred for racing. In order for the old mule to become a racehorse, he'd have to be reborn as a racehorse, and that's impossible.

Man, however, who is a spirit living in a body, *can* be reborn! His nature *can* be changed! He *can* become a new creature in Christ Jesus!

It doesn't matter how well-educated a man becomes, how many dollars he has, or how religious he is — mere man cannot stand in the Presence of God, because his nature is wrong.

Man is lost today not because of what he *does*, but because of what he *is*. (What he does is the result of what he is.) Man needs *life* from God, because he is spiritually *dead*. Thanks be to God,

Christ has redeemed us from spiritual death!

> **JOHN 5:26**
> **26 For as the Father hath life in himself; so hath he given to the Son to have life in himself.**

The new Man, Jesus Christ, had no death in Him. He was not born as we are born. He didn't have the spiritual nature of death — the devil — in Him. Yet Hebrews 2:9 says He tasted death for every man. He took upon Himself our sin nature. Hebrews 9:26 says He *". . . put away sin* [not sins] *by the sacrifice of himself."* He took upon Himself our sin nature, the nature of spiritual death, that we might have eternal life.

Jesus said, *"The thief* [the devil] *cometh not, but for to steal, and to kill, and to destroy: I am come that they might have life, and that they might have it more abundantly"* (John 10:10).

Jesus also said, *". . . I say unto you, He that heareth my word, and believeth on him that sent me, hath everlasting life, and shall not come into condemnation; but is passed from death unto life"* (John 5:24).

Jesus came to redeem us from spiritual death. Adam was banished from the tree of life through rejecting God's Word. But according to Revelation 2:7, all who now accept and obey the Word of God are brought back to the tree of life.

This *New Birth* does not take place gradually. It is instantaneous! It is a gift of God received the moment we believe.

Ephesians 2:1 says that you who were dead in trespasses and sins (that's spiritual death) He has quickened — made alive! Verses 8 and 9 tells us how it came about:

EPHESIANS 2:8,9
8 For by grace are ye saved through faith; and that not of yourselves: it is the gift of God:
9 Not of works, lest any man should boast.

Not of works. That punctures the balloon of the ego! Man wants to *do* something to save himself. He wants to have a part in it. But he can't. He simply must admit his helplessness and hopelessness. He must admit he is just what the Bible says — a lost sinner. Then he must come and accept the gift of redemption that Christ bought him.

ROMANS 8:14-16
14 For as many as are led by the Spirit of God, they are the sons of God.
15 For ye have not received the spirit of bondage again to fear; but ye have received the

Spirit of adoption, whereby we cry, Abba, Father.
16 The Spirit itself beareth witness with our spirit, that we are the children of God.

Have you passed from spiritual death to spiritual life? Is God your Father? Can you look up to heaven and say, "Father God"? Is His Spirit within your spirit bearing witness that you are a child of God? Do you have the Holy Spirit in your spirit crying, "Abba Father"?

You do if you are born again.

If you are not, accept Christ as your Savior today!

A Sinner's Prayer To Receive Jesus as Savior

Dear Heavenly Father,

I come to You in the Name of Jesus.

Your Word says, "*...him that cometh to me I will in no wise cast out*" (John 6:37),

So I know You won't cast me out, but You take me in,

And I thank You for it.

You said in Your Word, "*Whosoever shall call upon the name of the Lord shall be saved*" (Rom. 10:13).

I am calling on Your name,

So I know You have saved me now.

You also said, ". . . *if thou shalt confess with thy mouth the Lord Jesus, and shalt believe in thine heart that God hath raised him from the dead, thou shalt be saved. For with the heart man believeth unto righteousness; and*

*with the mouth confession is made
unto salvation"*
(Rom. 10:9,10).

I believe in my heart that Jesus
Christ is the Son of God.

I believe that He was raised from
the dead for my justification.

And I confess Him now as my Lord,

Because Your Word says, ". . .*with
the heart man believeth unto
righteousness. . .*" and I do believe
with my heart,

I have now become the righteousness of God in Christ (2 Cor. 5:21),

And I am saved!

Thank You, Lord!

Signed _____

Date _____

About the Author

The ministry of Kenneth E. Hagin has spanned more than sixty years since God miraculously healed him of a deformed heart and incurable blood disease at the age of 17. Today the scope of Kenneth Hagin Ministries is worldwide. The ministry's radio program, "Faith Seminar of the Air," is heard coast to coast in the U.S. and reaches more than 100 nations. Other outreaches include: *The Word of Faith*, a free monthly magazine; crusades, conducted nationwide; RHEMA Correspondence Bible School; RHEMA Bible Training Center; RHEMA Alumni Association and RHEMA Ministerial Association International; and a prison ministry.

RHEMA
Bible Training Center

*Providing
Skilled
Laborers
for the
End-Time
Harvest!*

Do you desire —

- to find and effectively fulfill God's plan for your life?
- to know how to "rightly divide the Word of truth"?
- to learn how to follow and flow with the Spirit of God?
- to run your God-given race with excellence and integrity?
- to become not only a laborer but a *skilled* laborer?

If so, then RHEMA Bible Training Center is here for you!

For a free video and full-color catalog, call:

**1-888-28-FAITH
(1-888-283-2484)**

To use our Internet address: http://www.rhema.org